THE UNICAMERAL AND YOU

Collaborating for the Common Good in Nebraska's Capitol

Amanda McGill Johnson

illustrated by Paula S. Wallace

Hardcover: 978-1-7360604-1-4
Paperback: 978-1-7360604-2-1
Kindle: 978-1-7360604-3-8
EPUB: 978-1-7360604-4-5
LCCN: 2020921481

Publishing services: Concierge Publishing Services

Printed in the USA
10 9 8 7 6 5 4 3 2 1

Pohan press

OMAHA, NEBRASKA

Every day, the Nebraska Capitol building sees visitors young and old. Today, Jack and Sophia are visiting.

Hello, I'm State Senator Johnson. One of the best parts of my job is showing kids what being a Senator is all about.

State Senators are a part of the legislative branch of government. Our role in government balances out the roles of the governor and the courts.

Welcome to the Capitol's beautiful rotunda. Here there is art showing the history and values of our state. Look how high the ceiling is!

We are also right outside where Nebraska's Unicameral meets.

"What's a unicameral?" asks Jack.

A unicameral legislature is one group of elected people who make laws. Laws are the rules that our community lives by.

Our state is special because in all other states, laws are made by two groups of elected people. One group is called the house and the other group is called the senate.

"I heard a ding. What does that mean?" asks Sophia.

It means it's time to check in, like when your teacher takes attendance at school.

This is the legislative chamber.
All 49 Senators are checking in
by turning on a light.

Senators come from all types of backgrounds. Some are farmers, some are teachers.

Some are young and some are grandparents.

Some own their own businesses or work at community organizations.

All senators want Nebraska to be the best place to live.

"What are the senators talking about?" asks Sophia.

Some are saying hi to each other, like you do when you see your friends. Others are talking about what they are working on today.

We are like a family, sometimes we agree, but sometimes we disagree.

The best senators know how to disagree and even fight, without being mean or nasty to each other.

"Sometimes Sophia and I fight, like over who gets the ball. But then we calm down and enjoy playing together again. Working together helps us win," says Jack.

Good example Jack! After senators disagree, we work together on other good ideas to meet our goals.

A second ding means that senators are starting to talk about bills. Bills describe the ideas senators have for new laws.

Bills cover many different topics. Some are about what you learn in school, others are about how to create jobs, and some are even about how fast people can drive on the interstate.

Many bills are ideas that everybody likes. When we disagree, we debate all of the details before voting on the bill. Senators use facts, stories, and values to convince others to support their ideas.

"Just like when we debate what would be the most fun group science project to do," said Jack.

Sometimes a bill doesn't get enough votes to pass. The senators who supported it are sad because they believe it's a good idea for our state.

But they don't give up. They keep bringing bills and ideas that they think are good to the Unicameral.

It's a good thing most debates end in compromise. Both sides get to include things that are important to them. Cooperation helps the bill get enough votes to pass and be sent to the governor for their approval.

"Sometimes, there is more than one way to go, and we try to find the way that makes the most sense for everyone," said Sophia.

Yes, like that! It sounds like you are learning how to work together.

Maybe you will be state
senators someday...
or even presidents!

> **Dedicated to Po, Han, and all the children and grandchildren of Nebraska legislators**

This book is also dedicated to the Unicameral Class of 2006. The honorable:

Greg Adams	John Harms
Brad Ashford	Russ Karpisek
Bill Avery	Steve Lathrop
Tom Carlson	John Nelson
Mark Christensen	Dave Pankonin
Danielle Conrad	Pete Pirsch
Cap Dierks	Kent Rogert
Annette Dubas	Norman Wallman
Tim Gay	Tom White
Tom Hansen	John Wightman

If you would like to learn more about Nebraska's Capitol and our Unicameral, visit the page made just for students and teachers at:

www.NebraskaLegislature.gov

Made in the USA
Monee, IL
10 February 2024

52700510R20021